AF727042

© 2026 by Kimberly Haidinger

All rights reserved.
No part of this publication may be reproduced, distributed, or transmitted in any form or by any means, including photocopying, recording, or other electronic or mechanical methods, without the prior written permission of the publisher, except in the case of brief quotations embodied in critical reviews and certain other noncommercial uses permitted by copyright law. For permission requests, write to the publisher at the address below.

Bannon River Books, LLC
www.BannonRiverBooks.com
Rutland, VT

For licensing requests, other permissions, and bulk orders, contact the publisher at:
info@BannonRiverBooks.com

For free book activities, author visits, and sustainability resources, contact the author at:
www.TheCarbonEmissionsProject.com

This is a work of non-fiction. While every effort has been made to ensure the accuracy of the information contained herein, the author and publisher assume no responsibility for errors, inaccuracies, omissions, or any consequences resulting from the use of this information.

Cover and book design by Arlene Soto, Intricate Designs

Library of Congress Control Number: 2026900649
Softcover ISBN: 978-1-971343-00-6
Hardcover ISBN: 978-1-971343-01-3

First Edition

Printed in the United States of America

a kid's guide to ECONOMIC ACTIVISM for THE CLIMATE

written by
Kimberly Haidinger

illustrated by
Luna Hansen

Bannon River Books
Rutland, VT

WELCOME

Hello! Thank you for picking up this book! We are a mother-daughter team of climate activists, working on a series of books just for kids like you. I write, and my daughter Luna creates the amazing illustrations. Along with our friends and family, Luna and I have spent the past few years talking (a lot!) about the world, the **climate crisis**, and what we can do to help. Perhaps like you, we have felt worried, but also determined and hopeful. We noticed that many climate efforts in the U.S. get stuck. So, we decided to focus on where we feel we can get **traction**, **movement**, and success towards a **net-zero** world. Can you guess where that is?

It is working with and teaching kids like YOU! That is right, you are one of the best chances we have for making positive change in the world. And you are not alone. We are inviting you to be part of a **grassroots economic movement**, a people-powered shift to help protect our planet. When we make smart choices about what we buy and how we use things, we send powerful messages to businesses and political leaders about what is important to us.

Here are a few easy ways to start:

- Learn about **economics** and how it affects our planet's health (that is what this book is for!).
- Start making small changes in what you use, buy, and throw away. (Our first book, *A Kid's Guide to Climate Activism*, has some great ideas to get you started!)
- Talk to your friends and family about what you are doing and why.
- Work together to bring these changes to your school, neighborhood, and community.

When we use our dollars like votes, we help create a better kind of **economy** - one that puts the planet first. We are so excited to have you on the team. Let's get started!

With Hope and Action,
Kimberly and Luna

www.TheCarbonEmissionsProject.com

How to have the best experience reading this book:

- We encourage you to read this book with your friends and family so that you can share ideas, exchange and develop thoughts, and organize action plans.
- Read it over a couple of days so you can take your time to discuss the different words and concepts.
- We hope this book helps you to grow your vocabulary, especially those words related to **economics**. Throughout this book, you will be introduced to our big concept words. You'll learn about what they mean and how they impact you.
- All the underlined words in the book are defined in the glossary section in the back. If an underlined word is confusing, just flip to the glossary and look for that word with its definition.
- With some of the bigger words, we have included some pronunciation help in parentheses so you can practice saying them correctly while reading.
- Keep a journal or a piece of paper with you while you read so that you can jot down ideas and notes.
- Throughout the book, friendly icons will help guide your thinking: **Sunny the Spark** lights up new ideas, **Curious Quinn** asks why they matter for climate change, and **Vista Vera**, our magnifying glass, helps you zoom out to see the bigger picture - so you can truly understand and use your new vocabulary.

Economics: (Ek-uh-nam-iks)

is the study of how people and countries use **resources** to make and share or sell goods and services. Examples of **resources** are: money, land, energy, and time. **Economics** is all about how things get made, who gets them, and why people make certain choices when they spend or save their money.

Macroeconomics: (mak-row-ek-uh-nam-iks)

looks at the **economics** of an entire country, as opposed to **microeconomics**, which looks more at individual choices around producing, buying, and selling.

Macroeconomics is important because it helps countries make big decisions about how to run their **economies**.

Leaders look at things like **gross domestic product (GDP)**, **unemployment**, **inflation**, and **international trade** to understand whether the **economy** is doing well or needs help.

These calculations guide major choices about **interest rates**, **taxes**, and how much the government spends on things like schools, roads, and even climate programs.

Gross Domestic Product (GDP):

is the total value of all the goods and services a country produces in a year. In **traditional economics**, countries aim for their **gross domestic product (GDP)** to grow every year because **growth** is often seen as an **indicator** that the country is doing well.

Here is the problem: **gross domestic product (GDP)** only measures **monetary** value. It does not tell us:

- If our air and water are clean,
- If we are using up our limited natural **resources** too quickly,
- If everyone has fair and **equitable** access to what they need, and
- If people are healthy and happy.

Focusing only on **gross domestic product (GDP)** is like getting a report card that shows only your grade for math and ignores everything else.

When it comes to climate and caring for the planet, we need to look at all the ways our **growth** is impacting things around us, the good and the bad, and not just the money numbers.

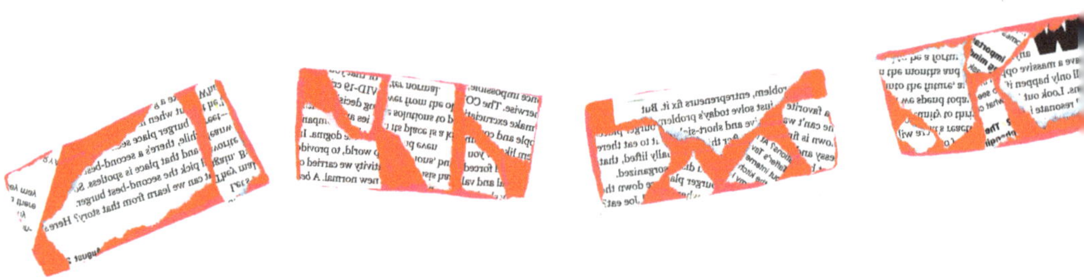

Why it matters for climate change!

Traditional macroeconomics and **gross domestic product (GDP)** are entirely focused on **growth**:

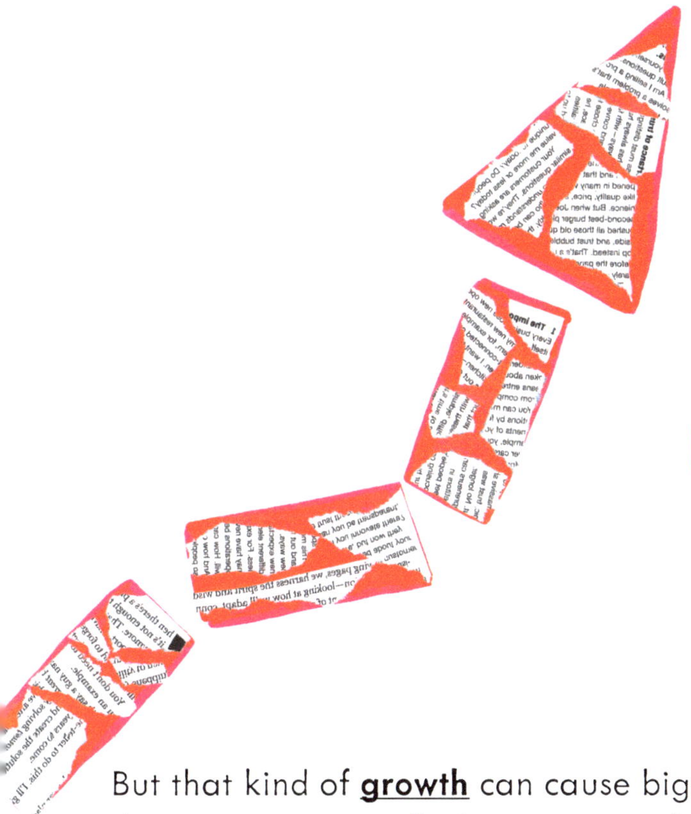

- More stuff
- More money
- More production

But that kind of **growth** can cause big problems for the planet. If **economic** decisions ignore **pollution**, **resource depletion**, **climate change**, and fairness, we end up with **policies** that harm people and the planet. So even if the **gross domestic product (GDP)** has increased and is deemed "healthy," it is not telling us the whole story.

That is why new thinkers (like you!) are pushing for a better system that focuses on climate-smart **economics**. It's an **analysis** that includes clean air, shared **resources**, and healthy people as signs of true success.

LET'S THINK!

Do you think "more" always means "better"?

(Hint: could "more" candy ever be too much?)

What other things, besides money, do you think are important for a healthy country?

(Hint: if you only had money, would you maybe be hungry, thirsty, cold, or lonely?)

If you were in charge of measuring a country's success, what would you include in your data?

(Hint: what are the things in your life that aren't *stuff*, but help make people happy and healthy?)

NOW LET'S ZOOM OUT!

All around the world, more and more people are starting to question the idea that endless **economic growth** is the goal. Why do we only measure success by how much money is being made, or not made? **Economists**, scientists, and young activists are talking about ways to measure progress that include clean air, fairness, strong communities, and a safe climate.

Some countries are even starting to create new tools to replace or improve **gross domestic product (GDP)** because, when we change what we measure, we can change what we do.

Capitalism: (kap-it-ul-iz-um)

is an **economic** system where people or companies, not the government, own most businesses, land, and **resources**.

In **capitalism**, people get to decide what to make, how much to sell it for, and what to buy.

Pros and Cons: **Capitalism** can lead to a lot of **innovative** ideas and products, but it can also cause problems if businesses focus more on making money than protecting people or the planet.

Socialism: (so-shul-iz-um)

is different from **capitalism**. In a **socialist economy**, the government (instead of individuals) controls many of the important **resources** and services, like land, factories, health care, and schools.

The idea of a **socialist economy** is to share things equally so that everyone gets what they need.

Capitalism is about individual choice and competition in business, while **socialism** is about cooperation and sharing things people rely on, like healthcare, schools, and homes.

LET'S THINK!

What do you think is more important, competition or cooperation?

Many people think we can *only* have **capitalism** or **socialism** in our country.

Is there a way we could have both– competition and cooperation?

Which economic system do you think would do a better job of protecting the environment?

Can you share some reasons why?

Could both system types be important?

NOW LET'S ZOOM OUT!

All around the world, countries use different mixes of **capitalism** and **socialism.** Most economies are a blend of both, not all one or the other. The government might run some services (like parks or schools) to make sure everyone has access, while private companies run things like grocery stores and restaurants, or sell things (like clothes or toys).

The important question is not which system is "better," but rather, how we can make an **economic** system that works best for people and the planet. As future voters, leaders, and decision-makers, you can help shape what kind of **economy** we all build next!

Supply and Demand:

The word **supply** refers to how many products and services are available.
The word **demand** speaks to how many people want to buy the product or service.

On this page, we show that we have a **supply** of one boxer puppy and two German shepherd puppies.

If two people want a boxer puppy, there is too much **demand** for what is available, but not enough **supply**. However, if only one person wants a German shepherd puppy, there is not enough **demand**, and there is too much **supply**.

FUN FACT!

The author and illustrator of this book (Kimberly and Luna) believe the **demand** for the boxer puppy is higher than the **demand** for German shepherd puppies. But they might be biased based on their own little boxer puppy named Vitus!

Supply and demand help decide how much things cost:

- When a lot of people want something, it has a high **demand**.
- If there is not much of it, it has a low **supply**:
  - This combination will cause the price to go up.
- When fewer people want something, it has a low **demand**.
- If there is a lot of it, it has a high **supply**:
  - This combination will make the price go down.

Here is an example:

If you shop for a bathing suit at the start of summer, lots of people want them (high **demand**), and there might not be many left in your size (low **supply**), so the bathing suit might be more expensive. The price has gone up because of **supply** and **demand**.

But if you shop for a bathing suit during a snowstorm or at the end of summer, few people are looking (low **demand**), and stores may have plenty, or have too many left over (high **supply**), so the price of the bathing suit drops to encourage people to buy.

Why it matters for climate change!

When a lot of people want the newest toy, gadget, or fashion item (high **demand**), companies rush to make more (increase **supply**). Making stuff means:

- Using **resources** like water, trees, land, **raw materials**, **fossil fuels**, and more,
- Creating more waste from packaging, shipping, and production, and
- Releasing more **pollution** into the air and water.

Even worse? Sometimes companies overestimate **demand** and make too much. After using up **resources** to produce a product, the leftover products may end up getting thrown away.

BUT WE CAN HELP!

When we make smarter choices about what we buy, we can keep the **demand** low for products that are less **sustainable**! That means less **pollution**, less waste, and more **sustainable** habits all around.

LET'S THINK!

Have you ever really wanted a trendy new toy, gadget, or fashion item?

Were you able to practice good sustainability habits and refuse that urge to buy?

Can you think of any products that you know are bad for the environment?

(Hint: can you think of anything made out of plastic or anything that is designed to be **single-use**?)

NOW LET'S ZOOM OUT!

Around the world, **supply** and **demand** drive huge industries like fashion, electronics, automobiles, construction, food, and more. When we all rush to buy the newest trend, it encourages companies to use more **resources**, even if it is not good for the planet.

We can slow down for a minute and ask ourselves:

- Do I really need this?
- Was this made in a way that is good for the Earth?
- Does this company act responsibly and operate **sustainably**?
- Do these questions make you rethink your buying habits?

Sometimes we do just need to get something!
When that's the case, we can use the power of our **demand** by buying from companies that care about the planet and work to create a cleaner, more **equitable** future.

Scarcity: (skair-si-tee)

means not having enough to meet all our wants or needs.

In both economics and nature, there are finite amounts of resources like:

- Money,
- Time,
- Clean water,
- Healthy soil,
- Energy from **fossil fuels**, and
- Trees, minerals, and land.

Think about a time when you got some money as a gift or saved up your allowance. You may have wanted to buy lots of things, but you only had money for some of the things. In this case, the **resource** with **scarcity** is your money.

You have to make choices about what you buy because you cannot have it all! So, even though there's a really cool new video game out, maybe you decide you have enough video games already, and you'd rather spend your money on a new experience like taking an art class, hosting a backyard picnic for friends or treating your nana to lunch.

That kind of decision-making is at the heart of **economics** - and you just made a smart one!

Thinking about **scarcity** and how we use our **resources** is also a big part of **ecology** and climate science.

Why it matters for climate change!

Like what might be in your piggy bank, the Earth has limited natural **resources**. Some **resources**, like oil, coal, and natural gas, take millions of years to form and cannot be replaced in our lifetime. Others, like water, forests, and clean air, are being used up or **polluted** faster than nature can renew them.

When we use too much too quickly, we create bigger problems like:

- **Pollution,**
- **Deforestation,**
- Water and food shortages,
- Species extinction,
- **Biodiversity** loss, and
- **Climate change**.

Understanding **scarcity** helps us make smarter choices, like:

- Reusing
- Reducing
- Refusing

This way, the things we depend on do not run out.

Life
Priority!
NATURE
beautiful
HAPPY
JOYFUL

LET'S THINK!

Can you think of something you use at home that may contribute to deforestation?

(Hint: where does paper come from? How about toilet paper and paper towels?)

Are there alternatives to the products that you use in your house that might be better for planet Earth?

(Hint: can you think of a single-use item that you could swap for a reusable one, or could use less of? Or, can you find similar products made out of recycled materials?)

Can you think of any ideas that may help to protect our planet's natural resources?

(Hint: is shopping second-hand or sharing with friends better than buying new?)

NOW LET'S ZOOM OUT!

Scarcity is a global issue. Countries, companies, and communities all have to make tough decisions about how to use limited **resources**. If we all keep **scarcity** in mind, we can plan wisely and make choices that protect the planet.

That is why **economic** activism for climate is so powerful. It helps us:

- To better understand the world's limitations,
- To live in a way that supports **equitable** distribution of resources, and
- To adopt habits that are **sustainable**.

Shareholders: (shair-hold-erz)

are anyone who owns a piece of a company or organization.

Shareholders have a say in how the company is run, usually by voting on important matters and company decisions.

Most **shareholders** are interested in making money. Sometimes this means they prioritize money over considering the **scarcity** of the **resources** they are using, as well as other potentially harmful environmental impacts.

Stakeholders: (steyk-hold-erz)

have an interest in an outcome of a business, school, or organization, but not necessarily the power to affect decisions.

You are a **stakeholder** in your school because you are a member of the community, and, for example, if the administration developed a new dress code **policy**, it would affect you.

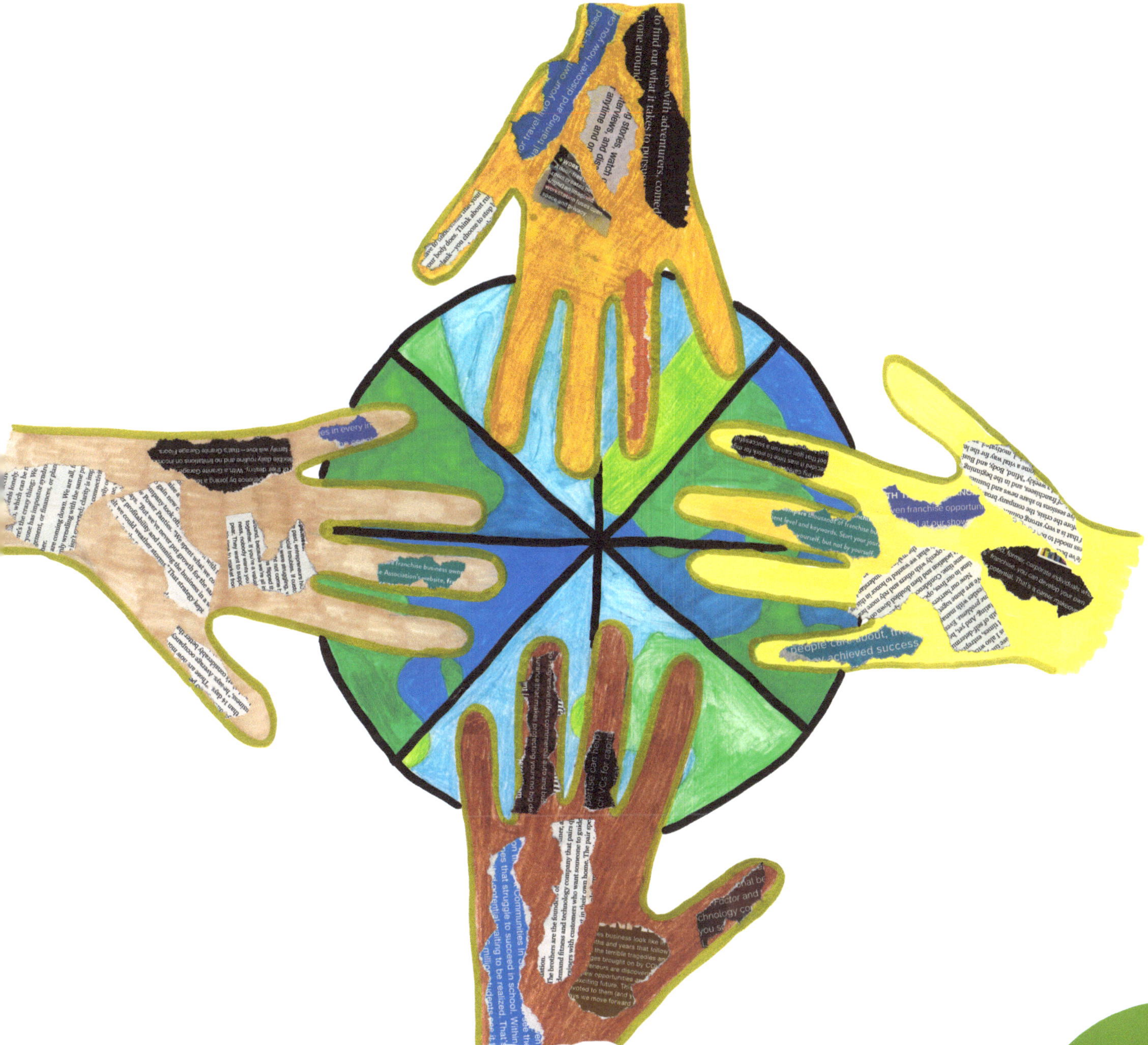

LET'S THINK!

Are there other communities where you are a stakeholder?
(Hint: what about your family?)

Have there been times when your family has made decisions without allowing you a vote?

Would you rather be a stakeholder or a shareholder? Why?

NOW LET'S ZOOM OUT!

- **Shareholders** get to vote on certain business decisions because they own part of the company. **Stakeholders** do not get a vote but are still impacted by what the company does.
- Common examples of **stakeholders** are workers, customers, and people in the community.
- All over the world, there are decisions being made that benefit **shareholders** while at the same time being detrimental to the **stakeholders** of the planet – that is all of us!

Assets:

are things you own that have financial value. That means they are worth money if you sell them.

Some examples of **assets** are your backpack, a pair of shoes, your basketball, a collection of books, a piggy bank with savings, or even a bike or scooter if you own one.

Liabilities: (Layu-bil-u-teez)

are things you owe, like **debts** or responsibilities that you have to pay back.

Some examples are if you borrow money from a friend, or your family takes out a loan to afford something they would like to own but don't have enough money for, or to buy a new car or house.

Debt: (det)

is the total amount of money a person, business, or country owes. Too much **debt** can make it hard to buy new things, invest in important needs, or allow you to have enough money to be okay from day to day. And when you are weighed down by **debt**, it becomes much harder to make choices that are good for people and the planet.

LET'S THINK!

What are your favorite personal assets?

(Hint: is there something you own that you really prefer not to lend out to anyone, maybe especially your younger sibling or neighbor?)

Do you have any liabilities?

(Hint: have you borrowed a book from a friend, or did someone lend you a few dollars last time you were shopping together?)

Do you think having assets, liabilities, or debts impacts any of your decision-making?

(Hint: if you owe a friend money, do you have to skip going out to the movies until you can pay them back?)

NOW LET'S ZOOM OUT!

Businesses have **assets** too, like buildings, trucks, or money in the bank. They also have **liabilities**, like loans, unpaid bills, or money owed to employees (payroll).

Countries also have **assets**, like natural **resources**, money, land, and public buildings. They also have **liabilities**, especially if they borrow money from other countries or organizations. This kind of **national debt** can make it harder for a country to invest in things like schools, health care, or even **climate change mitigation**.

That is why in **macroeconomics**, looking at a country's **assets** and **liabilities** is super important. It helps leaders understand how strong the **economy** is and what decisions they need to make next. Hopefully, leaders have climate health at the forefront of their minds!

Stranded Assets:

are **assets** that lose their monetary value. An **asset** can lose its value because of global changes like, for example, new climate laws or a drop in **demand** for **fossil fuels**.

Examples of **stranded assets** could be things like oil rigs, coal-burning power plants, or gas pipelines that were once important **infrastructure** for a company's activities. They are extremely expensive to build and maintain, and when they become **stranded assets**, for whatever reason, the company loses a lot of money.

When expensive **infrastructure** becomes a **stranded asset**, it starts costing money just to exist, instead of making money by being put to work.

Companies (and countries, too) don't want to lose money, and many will fight to protect their **assets** even if it is bad for the Earth!

Sunk Costs:

This is money that has already been spent on something that cannot be undone, even when it turns out to be a mistake. For example, a company builds a factory that eventually has to close because not enough people are buying the product made there anymore. The money used to build the factory is gone and is a **sunk cost**. The factory is now a **stranded asset**.

Why it matters for climate change!

Many big companies and governments have already spent billions of dollars on **infrastructure** that depends on the use of **fossil fuels**. Oil refineries, mines, and gas pipelines are only a part of it. A shift to cleaner energy like wind and solar would make any investment in **fossil fuels** useless. And in some cases, it is not just one part of a business, it is the whole business!

That means:

- **Stranded assets**
- **Sunk costs**
- **Liabilities**
- **Debts**, and
- Very unhappy **shareholders!**

SOS
SOS
SOS
SOS
SOS
SOS
SOS
SOS
SOS
SOS

LET'S THINK!

When you consider the pressure from **shareholders** and the financial risks businesses and countries face,

does it make sense why so many still prioritize growth and profits over the health of the planet?

Do you think there is a way to get shareholders to choose the planet over profits?

NOW LET'S ZOOM OUT!

This is a big deal for businesses and countries alike. Some have based their whole **economy** on **fossil fuels**. Switching to clean energy might feel impossible, scary, and expensive, but not switching could be worse. That is why smart climate action means making bold choices, even if it means leaving some things behind.

By understanding **stranded assets** and **sunk costs**, you can see why clinging to **growth**-focused **traditional economics** slows down our fight against **climate change**. And perhaps you also understand why it is so important for people who are *not* **shareholders** (as shareholders earn, or lose, money from **fossil fuels**) to be making **policy** decisions as we move toward an **economy** focused on climate health.

Profit and Loss:

is the money a **shareholder** or business gets to keep after paying all the costs of making and selling something. Here is a simple example:

If it costs a company $5.00 (in materials, equipment, payroll, and more) to make a reusable water bottle and they sell it for $10.00, the **profit** is $5.00.

But if it costs more to make something than the company earns from selling it, that is called a **loss.**

Most businesses are built to make a **profit**. But sometimes, trying to make as much **profit** as possible can lead to decisions that are not climate-friendly.

Check out the example from a lemonade stand on the next page.

- Can you figure out how much **profit** you can make if you sell your lemonade for $6.00 per cup?
- Are the assumptions reasonable? Can you create a **profit** and **loss** statement for a bake sale product, like, for instance, homemade brownies?

Why it matters for climate change!

To make more **profit**, some companies look for the cheapest materials or fastest ways to make things, even if that means:

- **Polluting** the air, soil, or water,
- Wasting natural **resources,**
- Underpaying workers,
- Using factories with unsafe conditions, and
- Ignoring environmental rules.

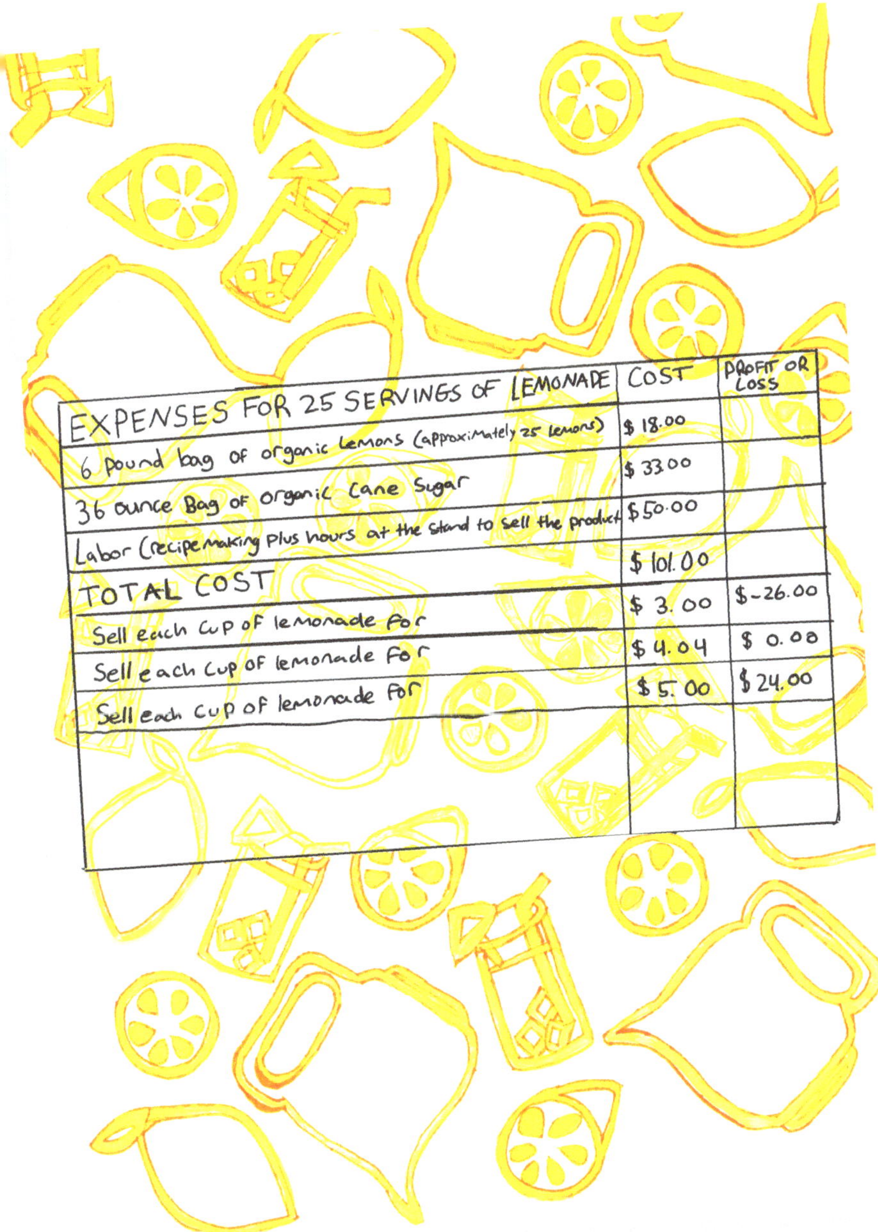

EXPENSES FOR 25 SERVINGS OF LEMONADE	COST	PROFIT OR LOSS
6 pound bag of organic lemons (approximately 25 lemons)	$ 18.00	
36 ounce Bag of organic Cane Sugar	$ 33.00	
Labor (recipe making plus hours at the stand to sell the product)	$ 50.00	
TOTAL COST	$ 101.00	
Sell each cup of lemonade for	$ 3.00	$ -26.00
Sell each cup of lemonade for	$ 4.04	$ 0.00
Sell each cup of lemonade for	$ 5.00	$ 24.00

When the main goal is **profit**, the planet often loses. But when businesses choose to care about people and the environment, even if it costs a little more, they help create a better future for everyone.

LET'S THINK!

Can you think of something that is super cheap to buy, but might not be good for the planet?

(Hint: think about all the little toys and trinkets you find by the check-out at so many stores that break quickly and end up getting thrown away.)

What do you think a company should care about more: profit or people?

Or is it possible to care about both?

Would you be willing to spend more money on something if you knew it was made in a way that is better for the environment?

For example:

1. You found an exciting new toy, but it costs every penny of your birthday money.
2. You found two toys that leave enough money for you to also buy an ice cream treat, but these cheaper toys were made in a way that harmed the environment.

What would you do?

NOW LET'S ZOOM OUT!

All around the world, big companies make choices based on **profit**. That means what we buy and where we shop really matters! When people start spending their money on products made in safe, fair, and more sustainable ways, companies take notice and change their behavior.

That is what **economic activism** is all about: using your dollars like votes to support the kind of world you want to live in.

Monopoly:

is when one company (or person) is the only one offering a product or service in a certain area. That means there is no competition, so the company can decide how much to charge and what kind of quality to provide. Often they choose higher prices and lower quality because they can, and it makes them the most **profit**. People who want or need that product do not have other choices, so they have to accept what the company offers.

Here is an example:

Charlotte is the only person in her neighborhood old enough to babysit. That means she has a **monopoly** on babysitting! If someone needs a sitter, Charlotte is the only option, and this allows her to set her own terms, like charging more per hour than if she had competition.

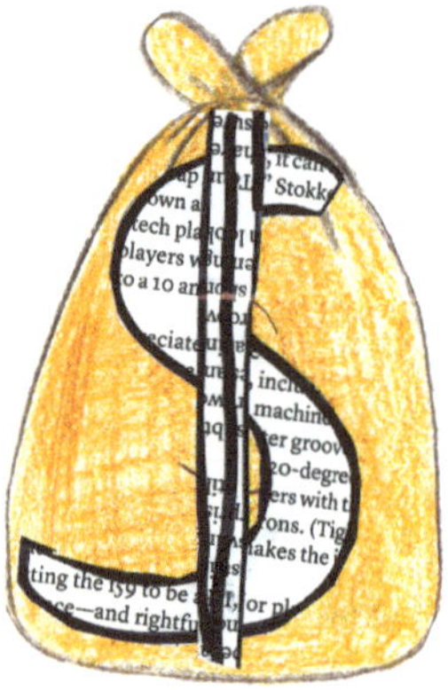

LET'S THINK!

Why might a monopoly be a good thing from Charlotte's perspective?

Would you like to have a business that is a monopoly, or do you prefer to have competition?

Can you think of any reasons why a monopoly could be a bad thing?

NOW LET'S ZOOM OUT!

When companies have this much control, they can raise prices or lower quality without losing customers because there is nowhere else to go. That is why many governments create rules to stop companies from becoming **monopolies**.

Too much power in one place can lead to unfair treatment for workers, customers, and even the planet. What if the only company selling shoes did not care about **pollution**? People would have to buy from them anyway!

Monopolies can affect not just what we pay, but also how businesses treat people and the environment.

That is why competition, choices, and smart rules really matter.

Sustainability: (sus-teyn-u-bil-itee)

The **United Nations** defines **sustainability** as, "meeting the needs of the present without compromising the ability of future generations to meet their own needs." (United Nations, n.d.)

Sustainability is an important word because the world cannot focus on what future generations need if its countries' **economies** are structured solely for **growth**.

Growth:

- Trying to make more and more.
- Sell more and more.
- Keep people buying more and more.

The result of all that "more and more" is:

- An increase in pollution,
- A greater depletion of resources, and
- A bigger problem with waste.

The Earth has limits. Instead of focusing on growing the **economy** no matter what, we need to shift our focus to **sustainable** decision-making and using different measurements for defining a successful **economy**.

The R's of Sustainability:

Arrrrrre you smart about sustainability? The R's of sustainability give us an easy way to remember that we can make choices about how we use stuff and spend our money.

When we follow the R's, we help shift the **economy** from one that takes too much and wastes too often to one that protects people and the planet. We have the power to build a future that is not about constant **growth**, but rather about caring for the Earth and each other.

Reduce

Refuse

Rethink

Reuse

Repair

Recycle

Reduce:

We cannot keep buying more and more while expecting the planet to keep up. Reducing means using and buying less. This is how we stop fueling a system built on endless **consumption** and start spending with purpose.

Refuse:

Say no to products and companies that hurt people or the planet. Refuse to buy **single-use items**, products made with **fossil fuels**, or anything designed to be thrown away. Your money is powerful. Refuse to give it to companies that cause harm.

Rethink:

Time to question everything!

- How is this product made?
- Where did it come from?
- Do I really need it?
- Is it built to last?

Rethink the idea that constant **growth** and more, more, more, equals success. Real success means clean air, healthy communities, and a livable planet. Redirect your dollars to companies that do good.

Reuse:

Use what you already have. Borrow, swap, or share instead of buying new. When we reuse, we slow down the cycle of take-make-throw away, and that is a win for both the planet and your wallet.

Repair:

Broken does not have to mean useless. Fix your stuff when you can. Learning to repair helps you to be more independent, saves money, and keeps things out of the landfill. Repairing can also be a fun activity you can do with friends!

Recycle:

Recycling is important, but it should be the last resort - not the first. Try the other R's first to reduce what you even need to recycle. When you can, choose items made from recycled materials and recycle properly to keep materials in use and out of landfills and oceans.

Climate Revolution:

The word *climate* refers to the Earth's long-term weather patterns, and right now, those patterns are changing because of **global warming** caused by **pollution** and **greenhouse gases (GHG)**.

The word *revolution* means a big, important shift, a powerful change in the way things are done.

So, a **climate revolution** means working together to change the way we live, shop, and use energy, so we can protect the planet and create a better future.

By placing our values about how we care for the planet over convenience and habit, we can help trigger large-scale **policy** changes, energy **infrastructure** development, and model new climate-friendly individual behaviors.

A **climate revolution** is a values-based consumer **movement** built on millions of tiny actions that add up to...

ONE GIANT LEAP FOR OUR WORLD!

Collective Action:

is when a group of people work together to achieve a common goal.

It means joining forces because one person can make a difference, but a group of people working together can create real, powerful change. For example, one person picking up litter helps, but if the whole school joins in, the entire neighborhood becomes cleaner and healthier!

Why it matters for climate change!

Big problems, like **climate change**, can feel too big for one person to fix. But when people team up, everything feels possible!

Examples of collective action include:

- A group of kids starting a recycling program at school,
- A school club implementing **food-waste** **composting** in the cafeteria,
- A sports team volunteering to promote reusable bags together,
- A whole grade of kids signing a petition asking the school to stop using **single-use items** for school lunches, and
- A neighborhood of families coming together and switching to clean energy.

Collective action can shift **demand**, pressure companies to do better, and even change laws.

LET'S THINK!

Have you ever worked together with a group of friends to solve a problem?

Why do you think people have more power together than alone?

What is one climate-friendly goal you want your school or community to work on as a team?

NOW LET'S ZOOM OUT!

Around the world, **collective action** has shaped history. From civil rights **movements** to women's suffrage, where women got together and fought for the right to vote, to the "School Strike for Climate" protests started by Greta Thunberg that inspired millions of kids around the world to take **collective action**. When people come together, they make governments and companies pay attention.

By joining your voice with others, you can help shape a world that is safer, cleaner, and more fair for everyone.

Leverage:

means using a small action or tool to create a bigger effect. It is like a superpower that helps you amplify your impact.

Think of a see-saw. If you sit on one end and push just a little, you can lift someone much heavier than you on the other side.

That is **leverage**!

Maybe you have a friend who is a good writer, and you are a good speaker. You can **leverage** each other's talents to give an exciting speech about climate action together.

Sometimes the problems facing our planet feel huge, but **leverage** helps us remember that even small actions can lead to tremendous change. And finding tools to make the work easier is important. Those "tools" can include people too!

When you combine **leverage** with **collective action**, your ability to influence change becomes massive. You do not have to be rich, famous, or powerful to make change; you just need to understand how to use your influence in smart ways.

With the right tools and teamwork,
your small voice can echo across the world.

Why it matters for climate change!

Here are a few ways **leverage** works in climate action:

- Changing how you spend your money can shift what companies make when **demand** for a product drops.
- Telling your friends about how they can help fight **climate change** can grow a **movement** when one voice becomes many.
- Sharing facts on a bulletin board at your school or local library can spread awareness way beyond your own friend-circle, or neighborhood.
- Making a speech at school about **climate change** and the importance of **sustainable consumerism** can help to educate your classmates and change their habits.
- Writing a letter to a leader might inspire a law that protects the environment.
- Start a project that helps others learn about **climate change** - just like this book! The illustrations you are enjoying are done by a kid just like you who cares about the planet.

If our artist Luna can do it, you can too!

What kind of project could you try to make?

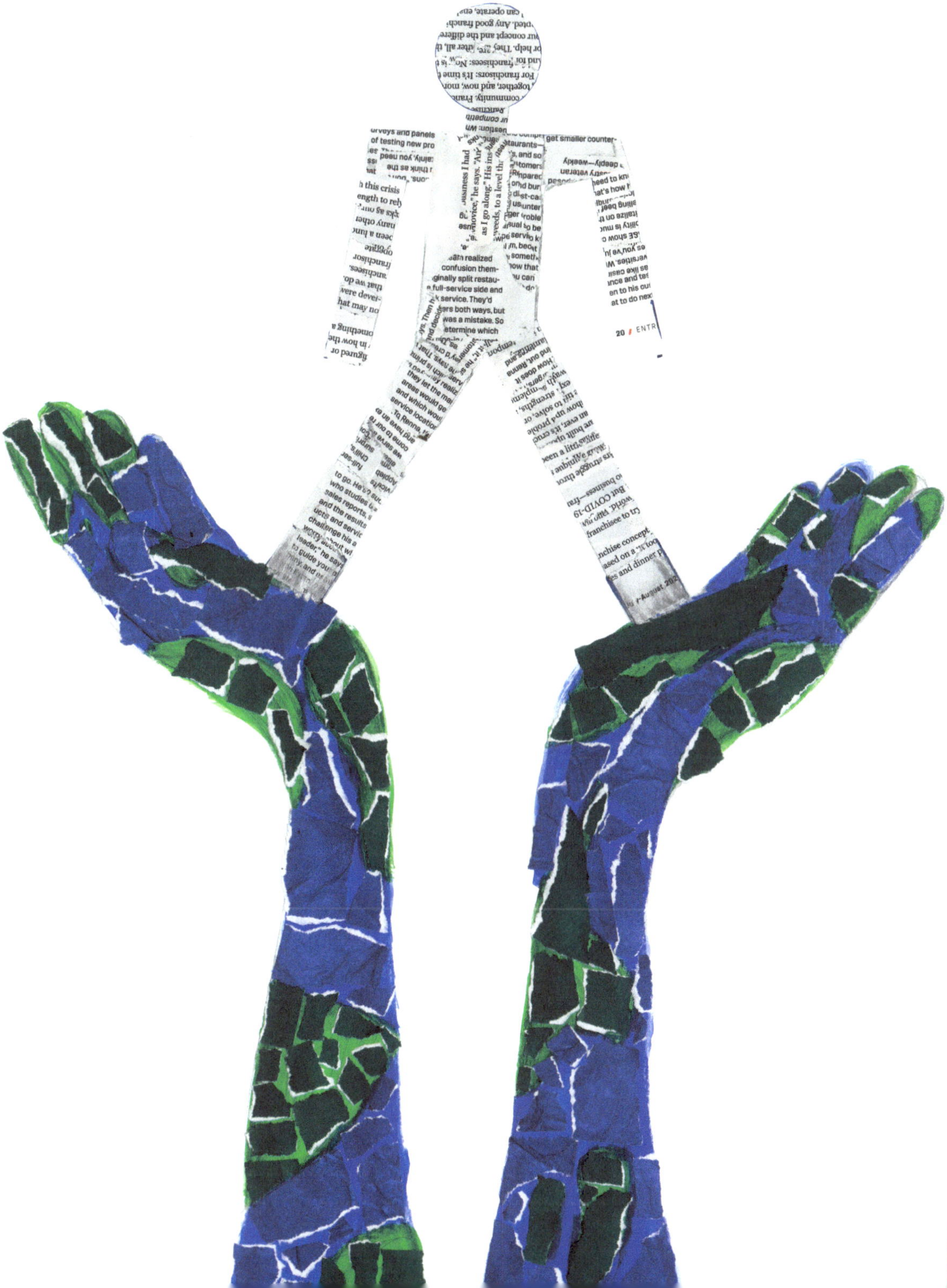

Boycott:

is when consumers refuse to purchase a particular product or actively stop shopping with a specific brand.

When we use our spending power wisely, we can help protect the planet!

Why it matters for climate change!

Why **boycott**? To send a strong message that says, "We do not support what you are doing." And when lots of people join in, it becomes a form of **collective action**. And you are finding a way to **leverage** your dollars!

Boycotts can get a company's attention, and fast! After all, as we have learned, if they are not making the money they expect, it can impact their **profit** and **loss**. Companies facing a **boycott** may experience reduced **profits**, potentially forcing them to adjust their business practices in order to address the consumer concerns that led to the **boycott**.

Many companies use materials and methods that hurt the planet by:

- Polluting water, soil, and air
- Cutting down forests
- Endangering **biodiversity**
- Creating waste

If they know people will stop buying from them because of these choices, they have a reason to change.

A successful boycott can lead to:

- Cleaner products,
- Less **pollution,**
- Less waste,
- Fairer treatment of workers, and
- Stronger environmental policies.

LET'S THINK!

If a company does something harmful to the environment, do you think it is fair to stop shopping there?

If you found out that the company made decisions that harmed the planet, how would you feel about boycotting your favorite brand or store?

NOW LET'S ZOOM OUT!

All over the world, people have used **boycotts** to demand justice for workers, for communities, and for the planet. In fact, some of the biggest changes in history started with customers simply saying, "We won't buy this anymore until you do better."

Boycotts show that consumers have power. When we stop supporting companies that harm the environment, and start supporting the ones that help, we shape a better future for everyone.

Market Disruption: (dis-rup-shun)

happens when the normal way a market works changes quickly and dramatically.

This can be caused by things like:

- A **boycott,**
- A sudden drop in **demand,**
- A big change in **supply,**
- A new law or regulation, or
- An unexpected event (like a natural disaster or pandemic).

Markets usually run in patterns with prices fluctuating based on **supply** and **demand**. But, when something unpredictable happens, those patterns can be disrupted.

A successful **boycott**, especially one focused on protecting the planet, can be a powerful form of **market disruption**. It shakes up the system and forces companies to pay attention.

Why it matters for climate change!

When lots of people stop buying something that harms the environment, like **single-use items** or **fast fashion**, companies lose **profits** and are pressured by their **shareholders** to change how they operate.

This kind of **disruption** shows that consumers have real power to make businesses more **sustainable**.

HOW DO ALL THESE WORDS COME TOGETHER?

While our planet struggles to recover from overuse and waste, many governments and companies continue to focus on **traditional economic** goals, like **gross domestic product (GDP) growth** to define success.

Shareholders worry more about **profits** than **sustainability**. They fear **loss**, **debt**, **liability**, **sunk costs**, and **stranded assets**. But what about the damage their goals cause? Even though **climate change** is better understood than ever before, many of these companies have not changed their practices. This tells us that some companies will not choose what is right for the planet over their **profits** unless we give them a reason.

So now it is up to us!

It is time for us to step up and **leverage** our power. By taking **collective action** with our voices and our spending, we can demand change.
We can spark a **climate revolution**.

Together we can **boycott** companies that ignore their impact on the environment and shift the rules of **supply** and **demand** by supporting businesses that care about **sustainability**. We can create **market disruption** and prove that the next generation of **stakeholders** refuses to accept business as usual. Businesses can either change now or risk being left behind as we demand a better future.

We are not powerless. We have big voices and big ideas, and the world needs to listen. We prioritize clean air and soil, safe water, and a healthy planet over **profits**, **pollution**, and **waste**.

Are you ready to begin your journey?

As the next generation, you are not just kids; you are the most important **stakeholders** on this planet! Show the world what that means for protecting the Earth!

It is time to let your climate beliefs guide how you shop. Start by paying attention to what businesses are doing. Some clues are easy to spot:

- What kind of products do they sell?
- Are they creating a lot of waste?
- Do their products last a long time?

To dig deeper, ask an adult to help you check the company's website:

- Do they have a section about **sustainability**?
- Are they supporting the health of the planet?
- Where are their products made?

It might seem like a lot at first, but soon you will discover brands that match your values and care about Earth like you do. Here are some simple tips to help you choose better:

- Look for products made from recycled materials.
- Choose items made locally or in countries with strong **sustainability** standards.
- Shop second-hand or find things that are repaired or repurposed.
- Check for verified environmental labels like Fair Trade Certified or B Corp. These mean that another company has checked to see that the product meets certain sustainability requirements.

Here are some more ideas:

Implement Change at School

- Start a **sustainability** club to tackle big ideas like:
    - Reducing **single-use items** in the cafeteria,
    - Asking for more plant-based lunch meals,
    - Starting a **composting** program,
    - Creating a recycling committee to improve paper and plastic recycling,
    - Developing a guide of climate-friendly brands that can be shared at a school assembly, or
    - Organizing a swap event for books, toys, and clothes to maximize the power of reusing!

Team-Up in Your Neighborhood

- Start a neighborhood group (online or in-person) that:
    - Hosts "Buy Less" challenges,
    - Shares tools, bikes, and **resources** instead of buying new,
    - Meets with clean energy providers to get better group pricing on solar and wind,
    - **Boycotts** polluting companies together, or
    - Writes letters to local leaders and businesses demanding change.

And even more ideas!

Take Action with Local Businesses

- Write letters asking local shops to switch to more sustainable packaging.
- Meet with restaurants and stores to encourage them to stop using:
  - Palm oil, which could lead to deforestation and biodiversity loss,
  - Virgin pulp toilet paper which means that it is made from newly harvested wood and contains no recycled materials, and
  - Single-use items like straws, paper napkins, plastic cups, and take-away containers.
- Promote and support businesses that are doing the right thing because climate heroes deserve recognition too!

Use Your Voice in the Community

- Attend town meetings and speak up for climate solutions like:
  - Clean energy,
  - **Composting** programs,
  - Green public transportation, and
  - Elimination of plastic shopping bags, straws, and other **single-use items**.

Here are some economic examples from around the world...

- The country of Wales signed into law the **Sustainable Development Goals (SDGs)**, making it an obligation for officials to pursue **sustainable** answers for development on behalf of future generations. It is called the "Well-being of Future Generations (Wales) Act 2015."
- The Wellbeing Economy Governments (WEGo), an alliance of the governments of Scotland, Iceland, New Zealand, Wales, and Finland. Canada is also actively participating. They have joined together under the idea that the **economy** should be serving the people and the planet first, with the focus on shifting away from **gross domestic product (GDP)** **growth** and towards wellbeing instead.
- The state of Maryland utilizes the Genuine Progress Indicator (GPI) as a way to include the state of social, environmental, and human welfare with its **economic** measurements.

For more ideas and an updated list of economic developments around the world, check out:

www.TheCarbonEmissionsProject.com

Glossary

Activism: taking action to make a change in the world.

Analysis: to break something down in order to closely study it or examine it.

Assets: something that you own that has monetary value.

Biodiversity: containing a variety of life.

Boycott: to protest a company by refusing to buy or use its product in hopes that you can bring about change.

Capitalism: an economic system based on private ownership.

Climate change: the weather pattern shifts caused by the increase in Earth's temperature due to a buildup of greenhouse gases (GHG) in the atmosphere.

Climate crisis: known as global warming or climate change, it is the long-term temperature change caused by human activities.

Climate revolution: a movement of actions taken to protect the planet.

Collective action: working together as a group, usually to solve a problem or achieve a common goal.

Composting: a process that turns food waste into a material that can be used to enrich the health of the soil.

Consumerism: the idea that buying more things is important for a good life.

Consumption: buying and using goods and services.

Data: a collection of factual information usually gathered through observation.

Debt: something that is owed to someone else.

Deforestation: the destruction of an area of trees.

Demand: describes how much people need or want something.

Depletion: using something up so that there is nothing left.

Ecology: the scientific study of how living things rely on each other for survival.

Economic(s): the study of how people use limited resources to get what they want and need. It includes the production, distribution, and consumption of goods and services.

Economy (Economies): a system of how a country, state, or other group manages its money, resources, and trade. (Economists: experts in economics.)

Equitable: being fair and just. It is different from equal.

Fast fashion: the mass production and sale of cheaply made clothing, sometimes even meant to be throw-away clothing.

Finite: having a limit, a limited number or quantity.

Food waste: food that is not eaten and gets thrown in the garbage.

Fossil fuels: are petroleum (oil), natural gas, and coal. Like fossils, they are formed from decayed organic remains.

Global warming: the process of our planet heating up.

Grassroots: a change that starts with everyday people, not leaders or politicians. It grows from the ground up.

Greenhouse gases (GHG): are gases in Earth's atmosphere that trap heat. The most common three are carbon dioxide, methane, and nitrous oxide.

Gross domestic product (GDP): the total value of goods and services produced in a country during one year.

Growth: Economic growth means that countries are producing more goods and services than measured in the previous year.

Indicator: a measurement clue, it points to or suggests something.

Inflation: represents an increase in prices. It means that the money that you have will not buy as much as it did before.

Infrastructure: includes systems of technology, facilities, and equipment that serve communities, like bridges, roads, and schools.

Innovative: new and original.

Interest rates: the cost associated with borrowing money or the reward for saving money.

International trade: the buying and selling of goods and services from one country to another.

Leverage: using a small action or tool to create a bigger effect.

Liabilities: debts or obligations that a person, company, or country owes.

Loss: when a business spends more money than it earns.

Macroeconomics: the study of a country's economy.

Market disruption: something that alters consumer behavior.

Microeconomics: the study of how individuals, households, and companies make decisions about spending.

Mitigation: to make something less, to minimize, or decrease the impacts of something negative.

Monetary: anything that pertains to money.

Monopoly: a situation in which one company or person has no competition in the sale of product or services.

Movement: a group of people working toward a shared goal.

National debt: the amount of money a government owes.

Net-zero: the amount of greenhouse gas (GHG) emissions and absorption or removals are equal.

Policy (Policies): is a set of rules or a plan that sets out a framework for how decisions are made.

Pollution: anything that makes the Earth's soil, air, or water dirty. (Polluted: to have made something dirty or harmful).

Profit: the money that is left over after all expenses are paid.

Raw materials: basic, unprocessed materials that can be found in nature.

Resource(s): a material or substance that is useful to people.

Scarcity (Scarce): when there is not enough to satisfy everyone's needs or wants.

Shareholder: a person who owns a piece of (a share of) a company.

Single-use (item): a product that is designed to be used once only and then thrown away.

Socialism: an economic, political, and social system based on government ownership and the belief that everyone should share equity. (Socialist: a person that believes in socialism.)

Stakeholder: an individual who has an interest in or can be affected by a company's decisions.

Stranded assets: something owned by a company that has unexpectedly lost its value.

Sunk costs: money that a business has spent on something that no longer has value.

Supply: the amount of something available for purchase.

Sustainability: protecting resources for future generations.

Sustainable (Sustainability): maintained, continued.

Sustainable Development Goals (SDGs): 17 goals adopted by the United Nations in 2015.

Taxes: money paid to the government by people and businesses to help pay for things like schools, roads, bridges, emergency services, and government salaries. Taxes are usually a percentage of the money earned or spent, so different people and companies pay different amounts.

Traction: describes the idea of surfaces gripping together to get movement.

Traditional: a way of thinking or behaving that is based on how something has been done for a very long time.

Unemployment: the measurement of people who would like to work but cannot find jobs. It is usually presented as a percentage.

United Nations (UN): an organization made up of almost all of the world's countries, established to create global cooperation and improve the world.

References:

Hayes, A. (2023, November 27). Genuine Progress Indicator (GPI): Definition, formula, vs. GDP. Investopedia. https://www.investopedia.com/terms/g/gpi.asp#:~:text=The%20genuine%20progress%20indicator%20(GPI,of%20green%20or%20social%20economics.

Wellbeing Economy Governments (WEGO): Wellbeing Economy Alliance. (n.d.). https://weall.org/wego

Meredith, S. (2023, January 2). The world's in a "polycrisis" — and these countries want to quash it by looking beyond GDP. CNBC. https://www.cnbc.com/2022/12/26/well-being-these-countries-are-looking-beyond-gdp-and-economic-growth.html

United Nations. (n.d.). Sustainability | United Nations. https://www.un.org/en/academic-impact/sustainability

Check out book 1 in the series:

For free book activities, author visits, and sustainability resources, visit:
www.TheCarbonEmissionsProject.com